CAREERS IN

USER EXPERIENCE (UX) DESIGN

WHY DO PEOPLE HAPPILY CAMP in line all night waiting for a chance to spend big bucks on the next iPhone? Why do we go to Starbucks when coffee is half the price at the local diner? The answer is simple. Design.

Every product is designed to be functional, whether it is a car, computer, or shoe. Companies know that customers will shell out more money for an experience that feels good. Customer-savvy companies (like Apple, Nike, and Tesla) that have invested in innovative design outperformed the S&P 500 by 288 percent over the past decade. That is the power of UX design.

Short for user experience, UX design is concerned with how a product feels, or more precisely, how it makes the end user feel. It is the most intangible part of a killer product. It targets the end user's underlying emotional needs while delivering exceptional functionality. Successful UX design creates an enjoyable experience that makes the lines between design and functionality disappear. UX designers work on more than digital products and electronics, like social media sites and smartphones. They work with all kinds of things, from airplane seats, to kitchen appliances, to hotel rooms.

UX design is now considered one of the best jobs in America with job growth of almost 20 percent annually, top pay well into six figures, and satisfying work that is both creative and intellectually challenging. It is one of the fastest growing fields with a job market that is exploding. The huge demand for UX designers is the result of companies realizing that profit margins can be driven much higher by creating an "I gotta have (at any cost)" mentality among consumers. Skilled UX designers are so highly coveted that they can choose to work as freelance consultants (for even more pay), or as full-time employees at just about any kind of company.

Nothing about this career is typical, not the entry requirements, the compensation, or the career path. There is no one traditional path to becoming a UX designer. Some UX designers start out as developers, others are art school graduates, while some have started with degrees in psychology, business, or computer science. It is desirable to have a degree in UX design, but it is not required. It is possible to start with no college at all – but that means self-educating through online schools and getting experience in the field through freelance work, internships, or volunteer gigs. What employers want to see is proof of your ability, and that is what you offer in a portfolio that showcases your work, whether paid or unpaid.

WHAT YOU CAN DO NOW

THE BEST HIGH SCHOOL CURRICULUM for an aspiring UX designer is broad. The basics include math, science, history, and language arts. Computer science is a must. Classes in psychology and learning to code will also be helpful. Challenge yourself with AP courses and sharpen your thinking skills with classes like debate and literary criticism.

Take some basic art classes to develop an eye for color, line, and perspective. Keep a sketch pad with you and draw out ideas that come to mind. Look for well-designed sites and products and try creating rough sketches of them. Look at each element and consider how it enhances the user experience.

In UX design, all knowledge is valuable. Read everything you can get your hands on. Read magazines, books, and newspapers. Read about history, business, art, psychology, statistics, science fiction, celebrities. It will all help you be a better UX designer.

Learn to use the software that will be your tools. Take an online introductory course in UX design. This will give you a good idea of what the work is all about. Do not expect this to be enough education and training to launch your career. Consider it a head start on your education.

Join clubs based on common interests like computers, coding, art, or anything else that interests you. The more you interact with people, the more you will understand what motivates them.

Get some experience any way you can. Your senior project could be building an interactive website for your school. Volunteer to design a site for a friend's small business or a local nonprofit. Be sure to include user surveys or conduct some user testing sessions.

HISTORY OF THE CAREER

USER EXPERIENCE (UX) DESIGN IS A NEW CAREER, having been recognized as a valuable profession in the late 20th century. However, its roots can be traced to the ancient science of ergonomics. The Greek words meaning "work" and "natural laws" were combined to describe a set of principles that would make work more comfortable, convenient, and efficient. It was ancient Greek physician, Hippocrates, who first used the principles to design an optimal surgeon's workplace.

Another ancient form of UX is feng shui. Developed in 3000 BC, this Chinese philosophical system aims to harmonize people with their surrounding environment. It is classified as physiognomy, the observation of appearances through formulas and calculations. While it deals primarily with real-world elements that one can touch and feel, rather than the virtual world most commonly associated with modern UX, it nevertheless shares many of the same ideas and goals.

The connection between ergonomics and UX survived into modern times. In 1900, a mechanical engineer named Frederick Winslow Taylor performed the first example of a systematic UX research. A leader of the Efficiency Movement, Taylor pioneered the idea of optimization of work, with research that studied the interaction between workers and their tools. Along with Henry Ford's pioneering mass-production techniques, Taylor shaped the early vision of what a desirable workplace should be like.

Reacting to criticism that Taylor's exclusive focus on efficiency allows measurable benefits to overshadow less quantifiable social benefits, manufacturers began to bring more humanization to the production system, beginning in about 1940. Toyota and Ford, in particular, valued engineering and production efficiency, but they also sought the input of their assembly workers. In fact, the blazing success of Toyota in the late 1940s was the result of encouraging workers' contributions of ideas that would make human interaction with technology less stressful, both physically and psychologically. Toyota's famous Human-Centered-Production system determined to improve efficiency by creating a more convenient and respectful environment for the workers.

For much of history, the effects of UX design were found in physical environments, but it was also in the 1940s that the future of user experience design emerged. That was when legendary English mathematician, Alan Turing, formulated the first theoretical computer. His *Theory of*

Computation opened the floodgates to the fledgling field of computer science, which eventually led to the countless smartphones and apps now carried in pockets around the world.

In 1955, American industrial designer, Henry Dreyfuss wrote *Designing for People.* This classic text pointed out that the successful design of a product was dependent on the connection between people and their experience with the product. He wrote that when the point of contact between the product and the user becomes a point of friction, the design fails. If, however, the design makes people more comfortable or just plain happier, the designer has succeeded. This idea was carried out in Disney's vision of the "role of joy." When announcing the development of Disney World in 1966, Walt Disney described the project as a place where imaginative use of technology could bring people joy. His philosophy of creating the happiest places on earth continues to inspire UX designers of all stripes.

In the 1970s, the era of personal computers started to take shape. Design was front and center right from the start. Xerox Parc (Palo Alto Research Center), the famous R&D lab in Silicon Valley, developed the computer mouse and the concept of GUI (graphical user interface, a way for humans to interact with computers using windows, icons, and menus). Under the leadership of Bob Taylor, a trained psychologist and engineer, PARC built some of the most important and enduring tools that gave form and function to the design of computers for everyday human use. Both Apple and Microsoft used PARC's work to develop their wildly successful personal computing systems.

The first UX professional was electrical engineer and cognitive scientist, Don Norman. In 1955 Norman was hired by Apple to help design its upcoming line of human-centered products. He asked to be called User Experience Architect, marking the first use of the term in a job title. Norman is commonly credited with putting the "user friendly" in Apple products. He is also known for writing the classic book, *The Design of Everyday Things*, which advocated for usable and functional design in equal proportion to aesthetics. The text remains hugely influential for designers today.

Personal computing blossomed in the 1980s and exploded with the introduction of the Web in the 1990s. This created a demand for computers that ordinary people could understand and use for their personal benefit and enjoyment. Graphical user interfaces, cognitive science, and designing for and with people became the foundation for the field of human-computer interaction (HCI). HCI popularized concepts like usability, and interaction design became the foundation of modern user experience.

In the Internet bubble of the late 20th century, new jobs with titles like Web designer, interaction designer, and information architect began showing up. As people became more experienced in these roles, a deeper and more nuanced understanding of the field of user experience began to develop.

At Macworld 2007, Steve Jobs unveiled the iPhone, a device that changed the design of mobile devices forever.

Until this moment, Apple had been struggling in the personal computer market. This singular product catapulted Apple into its current position as one of the world's most successful companies. The genius of the iPhone was in providing connectivity through a revolutionary capacitive touchscreen, which instantly made the physical keyboards of other phones obsolete. It was, and many think still is, the vastly more superior user experience of any product on the market, mobile or otherwise. The concept was so revolutionary it led to widespread business focus on user experience. It was hard to miss the market success and accolades that hurled Apple into the business world's stratosphere. Other businesses, even those not in the personal electronics sphere, wanted in on it.

Every step in the evolution of UX has involved an interaction between the physical world and human beings. As technology and the internet continue to dominate our lives, UX will continue to be increasingly important. The demand will grow for specialized skills in this multi-disciplinary profession, including user research, graphic design, customer advocacy, software development, and more. In fact, at any given moment today, there are more than 100,000 jobs for experienced UX designers. That number is sure to continue growing well into the future.

This field is quickly changing as it becomes increasingly important to the success of many more physical as well as virtual products. As a result, the job title UX Designer is in the process of evolving into Product Designer.

WHERE YOU WILL WORK

AS THE FIELD OF UX HAS GROWN, so has the array of employers from cutting-edge startups to well-established retail giants. Historically, the field has been most closely associated with large tech companies like Apple, Google, Facebook, or Microsoft. Companies like these employ significant numbers of in-house UX staff. As the importance of UX design became more obvious over the past decade or two, mid-size tech companies also began to grow sizeable UX teams.

Today, even the smallest startups recognize the value of good UX design, which may very well mean the difference between success and failure. Innovative UX design has even been used as a selling point for startups trying to raise funding. UX designers are therefore often among the earliest hires for startups. In the beginning phases, this may mean offering consulting contracts. The rule of thumb is generally building in-house UX design teams when a company reaches 50 total employees.

UX design is used in non-tech industries, too. Many companies have digital properties, but user-centered design can be applied to non-digital products and experiences as well. Today, UX designers can be found in the offices of traditional financial services, restaurant and hotel chains, apparel makers, entertainment providers, big box retailers, furniture companies, and just about every other industry that depends on attracting consumers.

UX designers can be direct hires or get their work through agencies. A third possibility is consulting. Self-employed consultants often command higher rates than their salaried counterparts, though they do have to cover the costs of their own benefits such as health insurance and business expenses.

Because UX design can be done remotely, you need not be restricted geographically. However, that advantage generally applies only to independent consultants. Most large employers who have UX designers on staff require work to be done on site (though a common perk is the opportunity to work from home one day a week).

The top 10 cities in the U.S. for UX designers are:

- New York, NY

- San Francisco, CA

- Atlanta, GA

- Chicago, IL

- San Jose, CA

- Seattle, WA

- Boston, MA

- Los Angeles, CA

- Charlotte, NC

- Washington, DC

THE WORK YOU WILL DO

UX DESIGN IS THE PROCESS OF CREATING enjoyable and personally relevant user experiences with products that may be virtual or physical with a virtual interface. Good UX design involves all aspects that relate to the end user, such as branding, design, usability, and function. The goal of a UX designer is to ensure that the product logically and intuitively flows from one step to the next. Every designer has a personal style and preferences and therefore there may be many different approaches to any UX project.

UX designers start with solid graphic design skills and a working knowledge of web and mobile technologies. In addition, they are expert in the use of a variety of tools. Some are standard design programs like Photoshop, Illustrator, Fireworks, and InVision. Others are more specific, like the wireframing tools, Axure RP and Balsamiq. With these tools, UX designers produce four major deliverables: a title page, an introduction to the feature, wireframes, and a version history. Depending on the type of project, multiple specification documents will also be included, such as flow models, cultural models, personas, user stories or scenarios, site audits, site maps, and any prior user research. All of this information, especially the annotated wireframes, gives the developers the necessary information they need to successfully code the project.

The UX Design Process

The first step in designing a product is to make sure the designers are on the same page as the business. This is usually accomplished through a series of brainstorming sessions that cover the why, what, and how of product use. The why considers the user's motivations for using the product. The what addresses the product's functionality, or what people can do with it. The how relates to the design of functionality that allows for ease of use in an aesthetically pleasing way. Once the designers understand the goals, they can start the process toward a final design.

The next step, and perhaps the most important step, is research. To attract and satisfy end users, designers need to find out as much as possible about people, processes, and competing products. There are a number of methods for accomplishing this. The main ones are surveys, focus groups, interviews (talking to actual users), competitive analysis, mental modeling, ethnographic research, and customer feedback and testing.

After research comes the design phase. Now the designer has to make sense of all the data collected. This is done through modeling of the users and their environments. A UX model is a framework that visually outlines the key components of user experience. Based on what has been learned about the users, the designer creates a persona, or more likely, several personas. Personas are composite archetypes based on behavior patterns uncovered during research. Personas provide designers a precise way of thinking and communicating about how groups of users behave, how they think, what they want to accomplish and why. Designers often name their personas, give them an avatar, and make them seem like a real person.

Next, the designer begins to sketch out the interaction framework, also known as wireframes. A wireframe could be a page schematic, screen blueprint, or other visual guide that represents the skeletal framework for the product. Their purpose is to indicate how to organize and arrange elements, establish an overall structure for product behavior, guide the product's flow, and generally show how to accomplish design goals. This phase can utilize various materials, from whiteboards to paper prototypes.

Once a solid and stable framework is established, wireframes are translated from sketched storyboards to full-resolution screens that depict the user interface at the pixel level. At this point, the development team is collaborating closely with the designer to ensure that the proposed design can and will be built.

The final phase of the design process is usability testing. It is vital that any product be thoroughly evaluated before making it "live." This is done by giving target users various tasks to perform on prototypes. All issues reported by users, whether good or bad, are reviewed and used to make changes in the design. After each change, the testing phase is repeated.

The UX designer title covers a range of roles and responsibilities. How much of the process a UX designer does depends largely on the type and size of the company. It is generally expected that a UX designer is a jack of all trades. In UX lingo, this is known as a "full-stack designer," which is someone who can perform any part of the design process from research through usability testing. In big companies such as Facebook, Amazon, or Google, design work is done by a team comprised of specific roles, such as UX researcher, information architect, or interaction designer. The following are the primary roles.

User research is a necessary component of every phase of the design process. UX researchers are focused entirely on the needs of the user. Surveys, interviews, market data research, and a number of other methods, are able to provide valuable insight into the behavior, motivations, and needs of users. UX researchers are mainstays at big companies, where the access to an abundance of data allows them to draw statistically significant conclusions.

Usability analysts evaluate interfaces already in existence. They use testing tools and research methods to determine what is working and where the interface falls short. Their findings provide actionable insights for future design improvements that could improve the end user's experience.

Information architects are responsible for a product's organization, navigation, and ultimate ease of use. They arrange information (content) and determine how it should be displayed to make it easy for users to understand and find what they are looking for.

Interaction designers are concerned with how a product feels and responds to a user. They provide transition effects and visual clues as to what is happening when a user touches the interface. For example, refreshing the mail app on an iPhone will produce a subtle bouncing animation. That gives the user a clue that the refresh is in progress.

Visual designers (graphic designers) turn wireframes and prototypes into visual designs that will be user friendly and will adhere to any and all brand guidelines. They are not concerned with functionality, but instead create visually attractive icons, controls, typography, and other visual elements.

As companies get smaller, the roles become more all-inclusive, meaning a UX designer is responsible for more of the entire design cycle. New designers typically start with smaller companies to obtain the experience in all parts of the process that bigger employers require. After a few years of experience, individual designers are able to steer their careers towards their favorite roles and industries or products.

UX PROS TELL THEIR OWN STORIES

I Started With No Degree

"I left my job at a real estate company because I wanted to do something creative that involved critical thinking. I didn't know what that might be until I read blogs and talked to numerous working professionals of all kinds. I asked them what their job exactly entailed and tried to imagine myself living their life. In the end, the core elements of UX design seemed to align with my notion of a perfect career.

For help building a portfolio, I enrolled in a 12-week UX bootcamp. No one should assume that a bootcamp is enough. After getting the basics down, it takes a lot of work to produce a few presentable design projects. I practiced a lot, redesigning all of my favorite websites, and then convinced a friend of a friend to let me design the interface of a mobile app for their startup. I was paid peanuts, but it counted as a 'real' job.

Looking back, I made it this far due to mentors and friends. Mentors gave me feedback and shortened my learning curve. Friends led me to jobs. Even though I work in a virtual world, living, breathing people are my best resources. All my jobs have come through friends of friends. Finding job openings is fast and easy. You submit your résumé and a link to your portfolio, but the portfolio has to be fierce. You'll get lots of rejections, but stay persistent. The door will open."

I Am a Digital Recruiter

"Experienced UX designers are always in high demand. Companies of all types and sizes are going through digital transformation to keep their customers happy. The result is that UX, and design-centric roles are among the top jobs in the US and the long-term outlook is excellent.

Want to know what UX employers are really looking for? It's all about your portfolio, which had better be great. All hiring managers want to see your whole process from start to finish. Each case study (design project) should include the team structure and your role, any personas that you created, and mockups. Think of it as a story that can help employers get a sense of how well you'd fit in their team.

My number one piece of advice is to make sure you maintain a current portfolio that showcases the top 10 percent of your most recent work. If you've been getting your jobs through people you know and not keeping your portfolio current, you are at a disadvantage when trying for a position where you don't have a connection. I would also advise playing up your people skills. Most employers really want to hire someone with a great personality, who is highly collaborative and can talk to everyone from the CEO to the UPS guy."

I Am a UX Design Manager for One of the Big Four

"What I get excited about is creating tools for people so they have a better day. That's been my focus for my entire career. As a leader, I have the power to actually make it happen. My job is to execute, and to choose and decide and ensure that the most important and meaningful features will be built.

I have a graphic design degree and a degree in computer science, so I'm both left brain and right brain. I found early on that art was not going to satisfy me intellectually and science was not going to fulfill me emotionally. I needed both. This led me to find user experience design before that term was even a thing. My first job was at a global engineering firm, where I was the first designer they ever hired.

Today, it is more important for a designer to have a business brain, so an MBA might be more appropriate than a computer science degree. The line between design and business is so blurry these days I can't even see it anymore. As you become more senior, business acumen is a requirement. Ten years ago people came from traditional graphic design programs. The next generation of designers is thinking business. That is a major shift among designers ages 22 to 30 these days."

PERSONAL QUALIFICATIONS

NOT EVERYONE CAN WORK AS A UX DESIGNER. It is an equally high-tech, high-touch profession. You need technical skills, and you need artistic aptitude. Working in UX requires you to not only love people, but to be endlessly curious about why they do the things they do. If you are not a people person, and you have no curiosity about human behavior, then this simply is not the career choice for you. Before deciding that you want to pursue a career as a UX designer, you must assess yourself as an individual and determine if it is something that truly does suit your personality. Take a closer look at some of the traits shared by the most successful UX designers.

Empathy UX design work means putting yourself in the place of users to understand their frustrations, fears, motivations, and joy. Good UX designers will never argue with the user's point of view. Their job is to provide the best possible experience for users, not try to change their minds or disagree with their opinions.

Curiosity about people is essential to doing the job right. The best UX designers are fascinated by the workings of the human mind and love to study human behavior. They are curious about all things that affect behavior, like culture, patterns, technology, and different environments. This curiosity is useful for pinpointing the right problems to work on, and creating the best solutions.

Communications skills are needed at every step. UX designers interact with target users online, on the phone, and in person. They also communicate with people with varying knowledge of UX design, from sales reps to CEOs. In many cases, they will need to explain what it is they do in language the average person can understand. Most importantly, they have to communicate effectively with the development team right from the start, often explaining precisely why something will or will not work.

Teamwork is essential in this field. No product is created by one person. UX designers work in collaboration with multiple team members toward a common goal. That means you have to get along well with others, treat team members with respect, welcome and accept input, and see criticism as a positive thing. You should also be receptive to feedback. Whether the feedback is good or bad, it is necessary to facilitate a good design.

Detail oriented designers make the work look simple. The best UX design takes place under the surface where the user cannot see all that makes it work. In reality, the work involves countless small interactions that make up the entire user experience. A good UX designer is able to keep track of the many little details it takes to create an entire experience.

Self-educating individuals make the best designers. UX design is advancing quickly. Those who succeed in this field are never satisfied with their level of knowledge or skills. They are willing to constantly learn new design techniques, new software tools, and new insights on user behavior. They are typically avid readers of every genre and subject.

ATTRACTIVE FEATURES

UX DESIGN HAS BEEN RANKED number 14 among the top 100 careers in America. There are a variety of reasons for this high placement, including rapid job growth, great pay, and satisfying work. It is meaningful work, too. UX designers get to work on a product from the inside out, making large numbers of people happy, while making a significant impact on businesses.

With an annual growth rate of 18 percent, UX design is

one of the fastest growing fields. It is not surprising when you look at just one small sector that depends on great design: smartphones and tablets. Every single interaction a person has with these devices has been heavily influenced by a UX designer. The result is skyrocketing sales. Smartphone sales alone grew 55 percent over a recent three-year period. Now nearly every single person in America old enough to swipe a screen owns one. Is it any wonder that the job opportunities for UX designers are booming? CNN estimates that a total of almost 3.5 million UX design jobs will be created in the US alone within the next 10 years. These jobs are not just in tech, but also in mature, blue chip industries like car manufacturing, hospitality, and medical services. That means there is a world of opportunities out there for UX designers.

UX design is fast becoming one of the highest paying jobs, especially in the tech industry. Even new hires with little experience can start out at $50,000 a year. With some experience, that can nearly triple, and in some high-priced areas like Southern California, salaries can reach $200,000 annually, or more. The picture gets even better when you consider it only takes four years of college (or equal alternative) to enter the field. Plus, the heavy demand for good UX designers has prompted employers to offer all kinds of cash incentives, like signing bonuses and stock options to entice the best talent.

UX is a great place for curious, smart people. It is highly interdisciplinary, providing chances to learn amazing things like cognitive science, anthropology, philosophy, and sociology. Along the way, UX designers meet new and interesting people, the kind of people that are fun to be around. There is no need to sit isolated in an office with your nose to the computer screen. UX teams are made up of all kinds of smart people. There are also opportunities to get in touch with large segments of the population through user research and user interviews.

The demand for UX design has made it possible to shift from full-time staff employment to freelancing. This offers a number of benefits. First is the chance to earn much higher income. The higher per hour income allows designers to fashion a work schedule that suits their personal needs. Many choose to work less and spend more time developing advanced skills – a move that pushes income even higher. Freelancers, often called consultants, typically have multiple clients. That keeps the projects fresh so the work never becomes tedious.

UNATTRACTIVE ASPECTS

IT SEEMS EVERYONE WANTS TO BE a UX DESIGNER these days for obvious reasons. For the visually oriented with technical ability, there is very little downside. Nevertheless, this career is not for everybody. First, you have to love everything tech. There comes a time in every UX designer's life when they say to themselves, "I don't want to see another device." There is an answer to that though. The Internet of Things and wear technology have opened up a whole world outside of smartphones and tablets.

Those who work for huge tech companies sometimes complain about being restricted to specific tasks when they would rather stretch their creative legs and work on other aspects of the UX design process. The answer to this might seem to be switching to a job in a small tech start-up where UX designers are given free rein to handle complete projects on their own. The downside to that scenario is the urgency to produce. Start-ups are a uniquely pressured environment, where employees are typically young and without outside responsibilities (families or social lives). It is customary to work long hours without complaint and without overtime pay to compensate.

These drawbacks explain why so many UX designers go out on their own at some point. Freelancing does have its perks, but it is not perfect either. There is no stable project source, especially when starting out, and therefore no regular paychecks or job security. Freelancers have to pay more attention to money management to get through times of no work. They also have to master the art of networking and marketing for new clients. It is like looking and interviewing for a job – all the time. Once up and running, the money can be great, but there are expenses that salaried designers do not have. For example, freelancers have to buy their own health insurance, contribute to their own retirement accounts, and pay for their own tools and overhead.

EDUCATION AND TRAINING

MOST GOOD UX DESIGN JOBS require a bachelor's degree. Previous design experience is usually required, but depending on the situation, demonstrable proof of skills may substitute. That said, there are no formal requirements mandating a certain degree, certification, or license. There are several ways to get the necessary knowledge and skills: college, self education, and online training.

College

Because this career is so complex, a good education is a must to become a UX designer. The work involves both hard skills and soft skills. It requires a high amount of technical knowledge, utilizing computer logic, coding, and other software-related skills. It requires an eye for design as well as knowledge of people, what motivates them and attracts them to different brands and apps.

At the very least, you need some type of post-high school education. It is possible to start with a two-year Associate of Arts degree, but keep in mind that some UX designers will have master's degrees or higher. Still, a two-year degree is a more convenient and affordable option for many students. Such a degree should be in a closely related field like graphic design or web design that will provide a foundation upon which you can start building your career knowledge.

For those who are serious about their future careers in UX design, a bachelor's degree should be considered a starting point. Unfortunately, there are not many universities that offer formal User Experience degree programs. The most well established include:

- Kent State – within its Library and Information Sciences department

- Bentley University – within the business school, it emphasizes the strategic role of UX in business.

- University of Washington – the Human Centered Design and Engineering program focuses on user experience research

- School of Visual Arts (NY) – offers an MFA program in interaction design with faculty that includes many well-known designers

It is not at all necessary to earn a degree in User Experience. It is quite acceptable to choose a closely related degree, such as communications, computer science, web programming, or information architecture. Design specific degrees in graphic design, UI design, visual design, or interaction design are also good choices. Some of the most successful UX designers have earned dual degrees.

The key is to choose the right combination of courses that cover both technical and design skills. Plus, UX design deals so heavily with how people think, a college curriculum should also include liberal arts topics like psychology or philosophy. In fact, typical minors for successful UX designers include anthropology, psychology, human-computer interaction, and sociology.

On top of a bachelor's degree, many ambitious UX designers have added a master's degree to their résumé. This advanced education is generally focused on obtaining cutting-edge software skills, delving deeper into understanding people's psychological responses, and generally solving problems related to the UX process.

Online training

If it is not possible for you to commit the time or money to a college degree program, there are a number of UX design courses available online. Not all of them offer certification, and most are relatively short in duration. The most popular ones that offer formal UX design programs that do conclude with certifications include:

- General Assembly – offers complete programs for full-time or part-time students that include both classes and workshops.

- DesignLab – is highly focused on design. The main advantage here is that the students are paired with experienced design mentors.

There are also numerous high-quality courses available, ranging from free to $99.

- Fundamentals of UX Design – from Tuts+ Web Design

- Lynda – access requires subscription starting

around $25 per month

- Udemy – some introductory courses are free, plus there is a variety of great supplemental courses for reasonable prices

- UX Apprentice – Free courses and learning materials that cover the basics

- Learnable – subscription covers access to all courses and downloadable ebooks and videos.

Self Education

UX designers need to be familiar with a wide variety of software and programs. A professional UX designer's tool belt includes:

- Wireframing and prototyping apps like Omnigraffle, UXPin, Invision, Axure, and Moqups.

- A/B testing tools test one or two elements on a page to gauge which gets the most activity.

- User feedback tools to gather more information from users. Survey Monkey and Mechanical Turk are general tools, while Usabilla or UserTesting are specific to UX.

- Web analytics tools like Google Analytics and KISSmetrics provide an understanding of visitor behavior and why users are converting (or not).

In addition to becoming familiar with the tools of the trade, mastering a variety of technical skills is a necessity.

These are the skills every UX professional possesses:

- Markup like HTML, XHTML, and XML

- CSS coding

- Page layout and interface design

- Image editing and production

- Front-end programming like JavaScript

- Information architecture, site mapping, and wireframing

- Usability testing and knowledge

- Graphic design

Additional skills that make UX designers more attractive to employers include:

- Project management

- Writing and editing

- Findability, search engine optimization, search engine marketing

- Accessibility testing and knowledge

In terms of importance, you need to understand the basics of user testing and be competent in wireframes and A/B testing. One of the best things you can do for your UX design career is to learn code. An understanding of HTML and CSS is one of the most vital components of the field because they act as the foundation or skeleton of a program.

This may sound like a lot to cover, but there are plenty of tutorials, courses, articles, and e-books scattered throughout the internet to help you out.

EARNINGS

THE DEMAND FOR UX DESIGN SKILLS IS HIGH, which puts job candidates at an advantage in salary negotiations. The average annual base salary of a UX Designer is just over $95,000, and the median is about $90,000 according to the most current salary guides. Salaries are good, but there are additional perks that sweeten the deal. For example, signing bonuses are commonly used to lure good talent. A signing bonus can be as little as $500 or as much as $12,000. Profit sharing and stock options are also common, particularly among startups that do not necessarily want to pay employees entirely in cash. The value of this perk is nearly impossible to predict. Some early joiners have become millionaires after an IPO goes public. Most, though, do not see much more than $10,000 a year. Still, it adds to the total compensation.

Earnings are heavily dependent on the type of employer. Large, established companies like Microsoft and Google pay much better than small startups or even established non-tech companies. These same well-paying employers are going to want only UX designers with solid experience. Poaching is common as they try to outbid each other for the best talent.

Experience is very important. The average starting salary for a junior UX designer is about $70,000. Those with no college degree and little real experience are more likely to be offered between $40,000 and $50,000. After three to five years, the salary typically moves up about $20,000. A UX designer with 10 years of experience can expect another bump of roughly $30,000. That is a total of almost $130,000 on average.

Designers in senior positions with more than 10 years of experience command salaries in the $150,000 to $175,000 range. After 20 years, most people have moved on to other jobs or established their own startups.

In addition to employer and experience, location can make a big difference. An experienced senior designer in the Silicon Valley can expect to do very well with a paycheck above $150,000 a year. Moving a few hundred miles south to the San Francisco area can mean an additional $100,000. It should be noted however, that where income is high, so is the cost of living.

OPPORTUNITIES

AMERICANS ARE BUSIER THAN EVER. Attention spans shorter. There are more methods for instantly comparing products than ever before in history. There is so much global competition, organizations cannot afford not to pay attention to design. The value of good design is undeniable: $1 invested in UX yields up to $100 in business. This has created a striking demand for creative types with technical skills.

The field of UX is experiencing double-digit growth that is unlikely to slow down anytime soon.

It is estimated that there are now roughly 500,000 UX designers employed in the US, and that another 100,000 will be hired within the coming decade. In an average month, more than 10,000 unique job postings are added to the online job boards. The range of employers is very diverse, showing that the need for good designers extends across all industries. A review of over 200,000 UX designers' online professional profiles revealed the names of more than almost 130,000 different companies that had used their services. Of course there were obvious big names like Apple and Google, but there were far more names that were far out of the tech field or virtually unknown altogether.

UX design is naturally central to tech, but the role has become so vital to the success of businesses across the board, the demand for these professionals is outpacing engineers and developers. A decade ago, there might be one designer on a team of 15 or 20 engineers. A recent survey of top designers found early-stage startups now have a design to engineer ratio greater than one in five. The average salary of UX designers now exceeds that of developers, more evidence of the importance of the UX designer in the tech environment. With advances in virtual reality, wear technology, and the Internet of Things, the demand for UX Designers is only going to increase.

Because this is such a fast moving field, there are ample opportunities for advancement for those with demonstrable skills. It is estimated that a junior UX designer in Silicon Valley, for example, will be promoted several times within 10 years. Each promotion comes with an increase in salary and a flood of contacts from hungry recruiters.

Unless you live in a very small rural community, there are likely UX jobs available in your neighborhood. Some locations are naturally better than others for the best positions. The top states for offering the most job opportunities are California, Texas, New York, Washington, and Georgia. There are naturally more jobs in metropolitan areas, and the demand for UX designers is greatest in cities like New York, Seattle, Atlanta, San Francisco, and Chicago.

Even if you live in a small town, you need not pack your bags for a trek to the nearest city. Most of this work is done electronically, and that means it can be done remotely from anywhere there is an internet connection.

Remote work is usually done by independent consultants, not salaried staff, but interestingly, the most popular way to work as a UX designer is through self-employment or freelancing. For anyone with the required skills and the ability to understand what customers want, it is well worth considering working as a self-employed designer.

There is no single path into a UX design career. Many of the current UX designers did not major in UX design in college. Instead, they came from other closely associated fields and gained the necessary skills for UX along the way. The opportunities are still greatest for graphic designers with technical skills. Consider that the estimated median salary for a graphic designer is $50,000, but common jobs for UX designers pay over $100,000. That means graphic designers who are currently working in print (and worried about their future) can more than double their income by taking the leap to digital.

GETTING STARTED

ONCE YOU HAVE LEARNED THE NECESSARY SKILLS, whether that is in college or through other means, the next step is to put this new-found knowledge into practice. In this field, your academic résumé takes a back seat to proof of ability. The first thing potential employers will be looking for is some type of hands on experience you have as a UX designer. There are a number of ways you can acquire this experience.

Internships are ideal for obtaining real-world experience. If you are in college, finding opportunities is easy. Simply go to your counselor or the campus career center and ask for help, but internships are not just for college students. Anyone can find an internship online through one of the big job boards. You will have to sift through all the internship posts that are directed at students, but there are plenty out there. This is a fast moving field. A year in an internship, learning the ropes as a UX designer, will have you well prepared for a real job.

Another way to get experience is through a short-term assignment on a real-life UX assignment. How do you do this as a complete novice? Volunteer. Tons of nonprofits cannot afford professional UX design and would love help with their sites and apps. Approach an agency and offer to work for free, doing some of the simple grunt work like conducting usability testing sessions or performing user interviews. It only takes a handful of these sessions to be ready for developing more advanced skills. If you know someone with a small business that could use some basic UX help, offer a freebie and add it to your résumé.

The next thing potential employers will want to see is a portfolio of your work. This can include school projects, volunteer work, or any other paid or non-paid projects that you have completed. Ideally, you will start out with at least three to six projects that showcase your skills. However, one solid comprehensive case study will be infinitely better than six projects that do not show process, narrative, or results. Even though your work will not be as easy to show as a graphic designer's work, you will still need to showcase your work in a visual way. Use sketches, wireframes, and photos of walls covered in diagrams and post-it notes. There are numerous sites that will allow you to put this together, such as Squarespace, Tumblr, and Carbonmade. Most importantly, be prepared to tell a story about the process you followed on a project during an interview.

It is important to establish a network early on. The key to future jobs is your relationships with established UX designers and developers. Meet them by attending as many networking events as you can. Naturally, you will also want to keep in touch with anyone you have met through internships or other working environments. There are also numerous design communities, like Designer News and r/user experience, where you can exchange ideas and make valuable contacts.

Get a mentor. If you do not know anyone who can fill this role, join the UXPA. In addition to plenty of industry information (like real salaries), the organization also provides mentorship through its local chapters.

If you invested in a college degree, you are in luck. There will be plenty of opportunities offered by your school's career center. Once you have graduated, you can expect alumni and recruiters to come knocking on your virtual door. Without this leg up, you will need to resort to looking on the job boards. General job boards will have some listings, but look for the more technically focused sites like Glassdoor, Dice, Crunchboard, and Stack-Overflow. Keep in mind that the best UX jobs, like all jobs, are not advertised. They come through LinkedIn,

Twitter, local event meetups, and referrals. Many are only ever sourced internally within the company and are never listed publically. Get connected and keep your online profiles up to date.

ASSOCIATIONS

■ **User Experience Professionals Association (UXPA)**
https://uxpa.org

■ **Interaction Design Association (IXDA)**
https://ixda.org

■ **American Institute of Graphic Arts (AIGA)**
https://www.aiga.org

PERIODICALS

■ **Smashing Magazine**
https://www.smashingmagazine.com

■ **UX Magazine**
http://uxmag.com

■ **UX Booth**
www.uxbooth.com

■ **Hacking UI**
http://hackingui.com

WEBSITES

■ **The Hipper Element**
http://thehipperelement.com

■ **LukeW**
https://www.lukew.com

■ **A List Apart**
http://alistapart.com

■ **UXPin**
https://www.uxpin.com/knowledge

www.ingramcontent.com/pod-product-compliance
Lightning Source LLC
Chambersburg PA
CBHW070905070326
40690CB00009B/1998